# BABEL WILL FALL

## Is the Church Ready?

Adam R. Hunter

# BABEL WILL FALL

*Is the Church Ready?*

## Adam R. Hunter

take heart books

# BABEL WILL FALL IS THE CHURCH READY?

Copyright © 2023 by Adam R. Hunter
All rights reserved. No part of this book may be reproduced or used in any manner without written permission of the copyright owner except for the use of quotations in a book review. For more information contact:
adamhunterwrites@yahoo.com
https://www.medium.com/@adamhunter_76

ISBN: 978-1-958818-07-7 (paperback)

Published by
Take Heart Books, LLC, Toledo, OH
Cover Design by Take Heart Books
Artwork by Canva

take heart books

Scripture quotations marked (NIV) are taken from the Holy Bible, New International Version®, NIV®. Copyright © 1973, 1978, 1984, 2011 by Biblica, Inc.™ Used by permission of Zondervan. All rights reserved worldwide. www.zondervan.com The "NIV" and "New International-al Version" are trademarks registered in the United States Patent and Trademark Office by Biblica, Inc.™

Scripture quotations marked (NLT) are taken from the Holy Bible, New Living Translation, copyright ©1996, 2004, 2015 by Tyndale House Foundation. Used by permission of Tyndale House Publishers, Carol Stream, Illinois 60188. All rights reserved.

Scripture quotations marked (ESV) are from the ESV® Bible (The Holy Bible, English Standard Version®), copyright © 2001 by Crossway, a publishing ministry of Good News Publishers. Used by permission. All rights reserved. The ESV text may not be quoted in any publication made available to the public by a Creative Commons license. The ESV may not be translated in whole or in part into any other language.

Scripture quotations marked (AMP) are taken from the Amplified Bible, Copyright © 2015 by The Lockman Foundation. Used by permission.

Scripture marked (NKJV) are taken from the New King James Version®. Copyright © 1982 by Thomas Nelson. Used by permission. All rights reserved.

Scripture quotations marked (KJV21) are taken from the 21ST CENTURY KING JAMES VERSION of the Bible. Copyright© 1994 by Deuel Enterprises, Inc. Used by Permission.

Although the publisher and the author have made every effort to ensure that the information in this book was correct at press time and while this publication is designed to provide accurate information in regard to the subject matter covered, the publisher and the author assume no responsibility for errors, inaccuracies, omissions, or any other inconsistencies herein and hereby disclaim any liability to any party for any loss, damage, or disruption caused by errors or omissions, whether such errors or omissions result from negligence, accident, or any other cause.

Do not be misled—you cannot mock the justice of God. You will always harvest what you plant. (Gal. 6:7 NLT)


Now all has been heard;
here is the conclusion of the matter:
Fear God and keep his commandments,
for this is the duty of all mankind.
For God will bring every deed into judgment,
including every hidden thing,
whether it is good or evil. (Ec. 12:13-14 NIV)


And they said to one another, "Come, let us make bricks, and burn them thoroughly." And they had brick for stone, and bitumen for mortar. Then they said, "Come, let us build ourselves a city and a tower with its top in the heavens, and let us make a name for ourselves, lest we be dispersed over the face of the whole earth." And the LORD came down to see the city and the tower, which the children of man had built. And the LORD said, "Behold, they are one people, and they have all one language, and this is only the beginning of what they will do. And nothing that they propose to do will now be impossible for them. Come, let us go down and there confuse their language, so that they may not understand one another's speech." So the LORD dispersed them from there over the face of all the earth, and they left off building the city. Therefore its name was called Babel, because there the LORD confused the language of all the earth. And from there the LORD dispersed them over the face of all the earth.
(Gen. 11:3-10 ESV)

# Contents

Foreword .................................................... iii
Preface ...................................................... v
Introduction ................................................ vii

## Part ONE                                    IX

<u>Chapters 1-4</u>
God or Genie? ................................................ 1
The 4,000 Year Leap: Information Technology and Artificial Intelligence ..... 5
Kings and Kingdoms .......................................... 12
AI: The Greatest Religion of Them All ........................ 18

## Part TWO                                    27

<u>Chapters 5-6</u>
Fear of Man or Faith in God? ................................ 29
Are We Ready? ............................................... 36

Endnotes .................................................... 43
Appendix .................................................... 47
Acknowledgements ............................................ 49
About Adam R. Hunter ........................................ 53

Is the Church Ready?

# *Foreword*
## by Dr. James Garrett

I AM HONORED TO WRITE THE FOREWORD FOR THIS AWESOME BOOK by my dear friend, Adam Hunter.

First, I have known Adam and his family for many years. I was their pastor for several of those. He is an individual who I trust and respect as a Christian brother and leader. I also consider him my friend.

Adam presented me with a draft of this message several months ago. He felt that he had received this from the Lord. I appreciate that about him because his desire was not simply to launch off on some tangent of an idea; he legitimately felt that he had received these thoughts, images, and words from the Lord for the purpose of disseminating them to a broader audience. His purpose was to draw attention to what is taking place around us, and to anticipate the future of the Church. He was seeking scholarly theological validation. For me, this writing was initially difficult to take in because it was a huge stretch beyond what has been normal consciousness for many Christian believers in 21st Century USA culture; we simply are not used to looking this closely and carefully at much of our context.

This work is a truthful and poignant illustration of the reality of this world. I know that many earlier writers drew "science fiction" allusions to Artificial Intelligence and similar ideas. I personally remember the movie, 2001: A Space Odyssey, and how its approach to AI created fear in many individuals.

The purpose in Adam's book is not to produce fear; it is to enable his readers to be aware that something dark is taking place in this world. I personally believe this book is prophetic in that it is preparing its readers for Christ's Second Coming, while showing all of us the realities being used to lead up to His Return. Again, this is not to be a fear-inducing work; it is to establish the Christian mindset to hope and to anticipate His Parousia.

I wholeheartedly endorse this book and my friend/author, Adam Hunter.

Please take the time to read it and pass it on to others.

*Dr. James Garrett*, DMin, MDiv, MMin, BS
Senior Pastor- Hope Church, Plain City, OH

Is the Church Ready?

## Preface

Yesterday, I put the finishing touches on this document. I'm amazed at how it all came together in the first place, and I can only credit God for making it happen. Although I have written many things throughout the years, this is my most ambitious undertaking since graduate school, especially considering the research and primary source citations I included; I wanted my warnings to be backed by evidence provided by those most directly tied to it. I pray that it made a difference in solidifying what I'm saying.

This message has been brewing inside me since 2021, and even before then in some ways. It took me two years to put enough puzzle pieces together to make sense of it all, and although I knew I wanted to write about it, I didn't know where to start. I felt prompted to begin by writing the scripture passages (listed before this preface) on which I base my statements and see what happens. After doing this simple task, my creative juices started flowing, and everything started coming together in ways I never expected but also in ways I'm pleased with. I completed this work in about two weeks.

The premise I'm offering is hard-hitting, direct, and specific. Although I may be addressing the Church, know that I am also preaching to the choir—namely, myself.

I was raised in a church tradition that proclaimed that the Holy Spirit continues to reveal Himself and transform lives, just as He did on His arrival at Pentecost. And although it believed the "1 Corinthians 12-14" spiritual giftings still applied to today's Church, the one most emphasized was the "greatest of these," love. The "lesser gifts," not discounted, were looked at cautiously by anyone claiming to be anointed in this way. In other words, you'd better be sure you're walking in the Spirit, not the Flesh.

With this internal caution, I present these prophetic words (although I feel so inadequate and strange categorizing them this way, except there's no other way to do so). In the past, I have been burned and confused by full-on charismatic manifestations, especially from fiery proclaimers and flamboyant manifesters; however, I've since started to understand that these "Signs and Wonders" are often—but not always—God-ordained, most notably from those who seek after meekness and humility instead of vanity and recognition.

Therefore, I encourage everyone to take my words with an open heart, mind, and proper discernment. If what I say here, in the end, proves wrong, know that I followed where I felt the Spirit led me and not some wild concoction or daydream I decided to run with. Also, the most significant point of this message is to call the Church to be ready for what's to come by being renewed and revived. Regardless of anything else, those truths come straight from the Bible, and I will stick by them 100%.

As I also tried to put forth, I have no idea how these "foresights" will come to pass other than believing they will. I try to keep any such conjecturing out of this piece and will leave such matters to those more intelligent than me.

Adam R. Hunter
August 15, 2023

Is the Church Ready?

# *Introduction*

AT A GOOD FRIDAY SERVICE IN 2021 and while in worship, I believe God spoke into my soul the words, "Babel will fall!" I was unsure what that meant, but I asked Him to reveal it to me. Slowly, He helped me put the puzzle pieces together (which I am the least capable of understanding.)

> This essay calls out Artificial Intelligence (AI) as the new Tower of Babel, especially those building it.

AI is proving to be a wrecking ball through society, surpassing mainstream technology with lightning speed. This year, especially, I have seen more options and availabilities for the general public to use tools like ChatGPT and other programs, allowing AI to simplify and be more efficient; its possibilities are endless. However, AI did not start on its own, nor is it being programmed by those who embrace mainstream western values. Instead, it's being overseen by Silicon Valley giants (many of whom are household names), who, although they may seem harmless, are anything but. The evidence is clear that most of them hold extremely progressive worldviews. Combined with their intellectual prowess and wealth, and quietly endorsed by world leaders, they see themselves as gods that will destroy anything in their way. Therefore, if you are a conservative or even a moderate, they will ensure that AI makes you conform to their likeness or that you will be obliterated.

If only left with these prospects, it would be deeply frightening; however, as Christians, we know how the story ends: Evil (namely, Satan) is defeated, and Good (namely, God) triumphs over all things. Just like it was in the Genesis account, God is not asleep at the wheel but is actively watching all that is taking place. He will not allow His Gospel message—or His people—to be usurped or stopped. The Bible says that the Gospel will go forth to all the Nations; it has not reached that point yet. Furthermore, it says that the gates of hell will not prevail against the Church. Christians will still be standing firm in the end. One day soon, God will stop this Tower of Babel building, along with its chess players concocting a scheme to reshape the world in their own image.

Without warning, this sequence of events will lead to worldwide chaos and panic. The only ones who will be at peace amid the storm are Christians. As others become desperate for peace and stability, God wants to raise His Church to show them the way. This will usher in a revival movement that rivals Pentecost, and countless individuals will come to faith in Jesus.

Although it may not be evident by human eyes, there is a deep spiritual battle going on right now. God is about to go nuclear on the enemy by toppling its Tower of Babel and is inviting the Church to take part in collecting its plunder—the plundering of souls into the Light of His goodness and grace. This will not be an easy task, but one that we are more than capable of through the power of the Holy Spirit.

The question, therefore, is one that we must account for without delay:

Babel will fall.

Is the Church ready?

# Part ONE

# Chapter ONE

## God or Genie?

"God is not a genie in a bottle, and your wish is not His command. His command better be your wish."
Mark Batterson, *The Circle Maker*

## The Vanity of Man

> [3] And they said to one another, "Come, let us make bricks, and burn them thoroughly." And they had brick for stone, and bitumen for mortar. [4] Then they said, "Come, let us build ourselves a city and a tower with its top in the heavens, and let us make a name for ourselves, lest we be dispersed over the face of the whole earth." [5] And the Lord came down to see the city and the tower, which the children of man had built. [6] And the Lord said, "Behold, they are one people, and they have all one language, and this is only the beginning of what they will do. And nothing that they propose to do will now be impossible for them. *(Gen. 11:3-6 ESV)*

From the dawn of creation until after Noah built his ark, everyone shared one language. They could think, create, and invent much more quickly. There were no communication barriers or massive amounts of people with their own opinions. They had learned to make fire, bricks, and buildings by then. They also knew how God rescued their ancestors from the flood but vainly said to themselves, *"That was a long time ago. Look at how far we've come as a civilization and all our progress! We're awesome, actually, and we deserve some Divine favor! We should 'make a name for ourselves' and build some tower (now known as a "ziggurat") to get God's attention. We could provide Him gifts and offerings there, and He would reward us with whatever we want! We deserve it, after all!"*[1]

Yeah, that didn't go so well. "And the Lord came down to see the city and the tower, which the **children of man** had built" (v. 5). (Emphasis added, noting the demotion from "Children of God" to "Children of Man"). "Behold, they are one people, and they have all one language, and this is only the beginning of what they will do. And nothing that they propose to do will now be impossible for them" (v. 6).

*"This is only the beginning. Nothing they propose to do will now be impossible."* What does that even mean, considering this was prehistoric times compared to our modern-day, 21st century living? Whatever it was, God knew He had to stop it quickly and dramatically.

## The Transcendence of God

⁷ Come, let us go down and there confuse their language, so that they may not understand one another's speech." ⁸ So the Lord dispersed them from there over the face of all the earth, and they left off building the city. ⁹ Therefore its name was called Babel, because there the Lord confused the language of all the earth. And from there the Lord dispersed them over the face of all the earth. *(Gen. 11:7-10 ESV)*

Can you imagine the confusion and chaos that transpired? One minute, these guys, on top of their games, were building something they thought would make them like gods or at least control God (e.g., *"making a name for themselves."*) They shared the same mindset, the same direction, the same goal, and, ultimately, the same language. Then, out of nowhere, WHAMO! They all started sounding like gibberish to each other. Ultimately, the genius, collective mind they once shared was no more. Talk about the "dumbing down" of society!

Although I'm only speculating here, I would imagine that before the Tower of Babel event, it was a good thing—a helpful thing for everyone to speak the same language. We wonder how those prehistoric cave dwellers figured out—for instance—how to make fire. Suppose everyone lived collectively and shared the same language, culture, and mindset. In that case, it's much easier to fathom how they might have figured out how to bring these things about. What started as good, therefore, ended up turning sour. The people's leaders became so powerful and narcissistic that they credited themselves solely for their societal achievements. They once saw God as a gift giver but started to feel He *owed them*. They thought they could usurp God by sitting on their own thrones and forcing Him to do their bidding. Instead, they learned a lesson that changed the course of history.

# Chapter TWO

# The 4,000 Year Leap:
## Information Technology and Artificial Intelligence

"To infinity, and beyond!"
Buzz Lightyear, *Toy Story*

Let's fast-forward a mere 4,000 years to today's 21st century existence.[2] In that period, we glided through the first eras of technological history.[3] After 1947, however, we launched warp speed into the digital age without looking back or turning back. I was born in 1976, and *I'm marveled by how far I've seen us come even in the last 50 years.* No longer are the days of rotary or push-button phones, landlines, VCRs, hard copy encyclopedias and dictionaries, card catalogs at libraries, cassette tapes, or players; these are just a few of the near-extinct creations that only a few decades ago were considered groundbreaking. Almost everything is becoming aligned with Information Technology, and almost anything you want to find out, see, or do is at the touch of a smart device or a command to Alexa. *(I'm not even going to bother explaining what Alexa is because, by now, it's a household name. Even more fascinating is when people call Alexa a "she" versus what it is—a machine.)*

Now, the new buzzword is Artificial Intelligence, better known as "AI," which is ". . .a machine's ability to replicate higher-order human cognitive functions, such as learning, reasoning, problem-solving, and natural language processing. In a system like this, its engineering goal is to design machines and software capable of intelligent behavior."[4]

AI is an amazing feat of technology, continues to evolve by the second, and is something I can't begin to comprehend.[5] Its algorithms, developed by the world's greatest scientists, have impacted our lives in ways we never realized. "AI is already around us in the form of computer control systems of many kinds, is now rapidly escalating with AI Large Language models like ChatGPT, and will accelerate very quickly from here."[6]

## Infinite Provisions?

Marc Andreessen co-owns a venture capital firm that funds cutting-edge technology companies. Not only does he invest loads of money in AI, but he also firmly believes that it is—literally—the only hope for the future. In his recently published article, "Why AI Will Save the World," he writes:

> What AI offers us is the opportunity to profoundly augment human intelligence to make all of these outcomes of intelligence . . . [such as] science, technology, math, physics, chemistry, medicine, energy, construction, transportation, communication, art, music, culture, philosophy, ethics, morality . . . from the creation of new medicines to ways to solve climate change to technologies to reach the stars—much, much better from here.[7]

He goes onto further explain what AI will provide all of us (with emphasis added):

- *Every child* will have an AI tutor that is *infinitely* patient, *infinitely* compassionate, *infinitely* knowledgeable, *infinitely* helpful. The AI tutor will be **by each child's side** *every step of their development*, helping them maximize their potential with the machine version of *infinite* love.
- *Every* person will have an AI assistant/coach/mentor/trainer/advisor/therapist that is *infinitely* patient, *infinitely* compassionate, *infinitely*

knowledgeable, and *infinitely* helpful. The AI assistant *will be present through all of life's opportunities* and challenges, *maximizing every person's outcomes.*

- *Every* scientist will have an AI assistant/collaborator/partner that will *greatly expand* their scope of *scientific research and achievement. Every* artist, *every* engineer, *every* businessperson, *every* doctor, *every* caregiver will *have the same* in their worlds.
- *Every* leader of people – CEO, government official, nonprofit president, athletic coach, teacher – **will have the same.** The magnification effects of better decisions by leaders across the people they lead are *enormous,* so *this intelligence augmentation may be the most important of all*.
- Productivity growth throughout the economy will *accelerate dramatically,* driving economic growth, creation of new industries, creation of new jobs, and wage growth, and resulting in a **new era of heightened material prosperity** across the planet.
- *Scientific breakthroughs and new technologies and medicines will dramatically expand,* as AI helps us further decode the laws of nature and harvest them for our benefit.
- **The creative arts will enter a golden age**, as AI-augmented artists, musicians, writers, and filmmakers **gain the ability to realize their** *visions far faster and at greater scale than ever before.*
- We will be able to take on new challenges that have been impossible to tackle without AI, from **curing** *all* **diseases to** *achieving interstellar travel*.
- And this isn't just about intelligence! **Perhaps the most underestimated quality of AI is how** *human-*

*izing* **it can be.** AI art gives people who otherwise lack technical skills the freedom to create and share their artistic ideas. **Talking to an empathetic *AI friend really does improve* their ability to handle adversity.** And **AI medical chatbots are *already* more empathetic than their *human* counterparts.** Rather than making the world harsher and more mechanistic, ***infinitely* patient** and *sympathetic* **AI will make the world *warmer* and *nicer.***

- The stakes here are high. The opportunities are profound. **AI is quite possibly the most important – and best –** *thing our civilization has ever created*, certainly on par with electricity and microchips, and probably beyond those.

Did you catch how often he used the word "infinitely," along with other noted utopian descriptors? Accordingly, AI will solve the world's most significant problems and be our best friend, teacher, therapist, and parent. Even creative artists will produce far greater works than could ever be imagined for all of us to enjoy. It sounds like heaven on earth. *It sounds like God, created by humans for humanity's benefit.*

## Frightening Scenarios

Despite his seemingly religious fervor about AI, Andreessen did address some significant risks: "The tip-off to the nature of the AI societal risk claim is its own term, 'AI Alignment.' Alignment with what? Human values? Whose human values? Ah, that's where things get tricky."[8] He discusses AI's programmed biases, its definition of harmful content, and how its opponents are frightened it becoming "a new kind of fused government-corporate-academic authoritarian speech dictatorship ripped straight from the pages of George Orwell's 1984."

> Once a framework for restricting even egregiously terrible content is in place—for example, for hate speech, a specific hurtful word, or for misinformation, obviously false claims like "the Pope is dead"—a shockingly **broad range of government agencies and activist pressure groups and nongovernmental entities will kick into gear and demand ever greater levels of censorship and suppression of whatever speech they view as threatening to society and/or their own personal preferences. They will do this up to and including in ways that are nakedly <u>felony crimes</u>.** This cycle in practice can run apparently forever, with the enthusiastic support of authoritarian hall monitors installed throughout our elite power structures. This has been cascading for a decade in social media and with only certain exceptions, continues to get more fervent all the time.[9] (Emphasis added.)

Then, with bold caution, Andreessen urges that society "[not] let the thought police suppress AI":

> If you don't agree with the prevailing niche morality that is being imposed on both social media and AI via ever-intensifying speech codes, **you should also realize that the fight over what AI is allowed to say/generate will be even more important—by *a lot*—than the fight over social media censorship.** <u>*AI is*</u>

*<u>highly likely to be the control layer for everything in the world. How it is allowed to operate is going to matter perhaps more than anything else has ever mattered. You should be aware of how a small and isolated coterie of partisan social engineers are trying to determine that right now, under the cover of the age-old claim that they are protecting you.</u>* (Emphasis added.)

I highly recommend anyone interested to read Andreesen's essay on AI in full. Although written in the fervor of an evangelist, proclaiming the "Good News of AI", his argument on how AI is charted to shape the future is well-stated. What would seem counter-intuitive, however, despite all his acclimations, is his stark warnings (as noted above) on how those in power are hellbent on using this tool to manipulate, coerce, suppress, and even persecute. His solution, however, is not to throw the baby out with the bathwater; there are too many rewards to be lost, and if the freedom-loving West does not seize the day, the Chinese Communist Party will.[10] Instead, we should ensure there are *<u>technological safeguards in place to keep the global elites from using AI to rule the world.</u>*

# Chapter THREE
## Kings and Kingdoms

"Poor man wanna be rich, rich man wanna be king,
and a king ain't satisfied til he rules everything."
Bruce Springsteen, "Badlands,"
Darkness on the Edge of Town

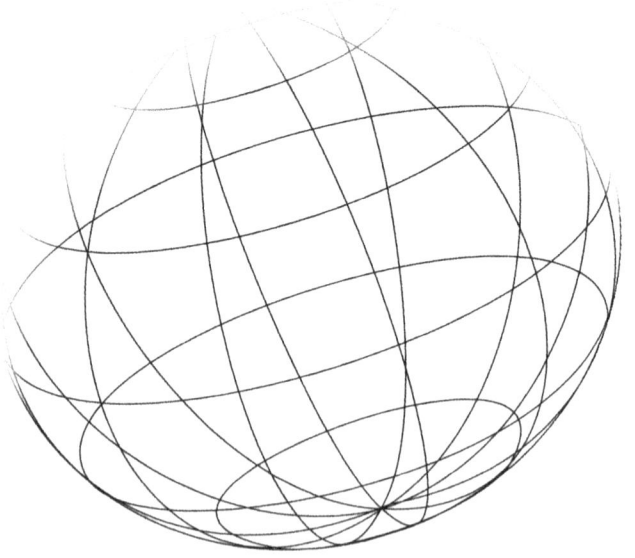

## Is the Church Ready?

But are safeguards even possible?

This is already proven to be fallacious with Meta, Amazon, Alphabet, Microsoft, and Apple corporate giants. Their CEOs and insiders (or, as Andreessen called them, "a small and isolated coterie of partisan social engineers"[11]), driven by their lust for godlike status, fueled by their unlimited income sources, and backed by the world's highest powerbrokers, have already made considerable strides in influencing public opinion, seeding chaos and division, and influencing elections. They may talk a fair game on the value of objectivity and freedom of speech, but in reality, they aren't going to regulate themselves.

Furthermore, if they hold the operational strings and their endless money supply is being funded by "kings and kingdoms" who also want part of the action, nothing will change; it will only worsen.[12] Rules, regulations, and laws are only as good as those enforcing them. **The only reason America's just legal system has flourished for two centuries is because those in charge—despite how morally corrupt they might have been individually—were still influenced by America's founding on Judeo-Christian truths. Horrifically, that influence is almost as good as gone, and unless things miraculously change, there will soon be no more.**

### Who's Running the Show?

AI could be the most beneficial thing ever invented, and it is already proving itself to be in some ways. In fact, it is even being utilized by Christian organizations to help spread the Gospel more broadly, effectively, and efficiently. As long as the doors remain open, God may use this technology to spread His good news throughout the 10/40 window, especially to those who still have no knowledge of Him.[13]

However, it could also be terrifying, depending on who enters the algorithms. If you think of AI as you would human development, a person's early childhood experiences often shape their overall personality schemas and futures. For instance, sociologists have repeatedly proven that children from stable, nuclear, two-parent households do better overall than those not afforded these opportunities. This fact draws itself from Judeo-Christian values and Biblical teachings of family structure. More than that, however, are children who are raised in the Church; even more, those who are instructed in the Bible's truths and watch them live out among others. Proverbs 22:6 says, "Train up a child in the way he should go, and in the end he will not depart from it" (KJV21). Of course, this does not mean that every child raised in a Christian environment will follow Jesus their whole lives; (although, as sociologists again have proven, it is much more likely than for those not raised in such environments.) On a broader scale, however, it does mean that those "chunks of wisdom" learned in childhood on right living will be embedded in that person's psyche. It's up to them, as free moral agents, what they do with it.

Devastatingly, most AI developers embrace a secularly humanistic worldview. They believe ". . . that a human is only a brain, no different from a computer. [Therefore, it] presumes (1) evolution, (2) non-existence of God, and (3) humanity as no different from objects."[14] *New York Times* technology columnist Farhad Manjoo provided an even more detailed accounting of Silicon Valley's core values based on a 2017 Sanford University detailed study of 600 of the "tech industry's 'elites'—not rank and file workers, but the millionaire and billionaire founders and executives who are best positioned to influence politics [and] guide policy as they and their industries grow as a political force."[15] Manjoo reported:

The study showed that tech entrepreneurs are very liberal—among some of the most left-leaning Democrats you can find. They are overwhelmingly in favor of economic policies that redistribute wealth, including higher taxes on rich people and lots of social services for the poor, including universal health care. Their outlook is cosmopolitan and globalist—they support free trade and more open immigration, and they score low on measures of "racial resentment." They oppose restrictions on abortion, favor gay rights, support gun control, and oppose the death penalty.[16]

So, overall, the "geeks of Silicon Valley"—the AI programmers—view life through a much more progressive lens than most within orthodox Christianity or, even more broadly, the millions scattered throughout America's heartland. If, like parents, these technologists influence their AI's "clean slate" by entering data based upon their antithesis toward Christian virtues, how do we expect things to turn out eventually? Not good; not good at all.

Even more, these technological power brokers genuinely believe *they alone* hold the keys to the kingdom. In the past, people have based their ethics and morals on religious texts and common laws. However, with this coming age of technology, they believe that those old ideals should be placed in the dustbin of history, having only held society back from actual progress into transcendence. To them, "following the science" proves that the ends justify the means and that "things are right and good if they have practical outcomes for the majority of people."[17]

## Follow the Scientists?

Civil Rights Attorney Noah Baron tells a story of attending a gathering soon after moving to San Francisco:[18]

> A friend took me to a party of people who work in tech. One of them insisted to me that China's single-party government is superior to American democracy because it is "more efficient." In response to my insistence that, though imperfect, American democracy preserves many of our political freedoms and secures rights of workers to an extent unknown in China, he pointed to the "massive" growth of the Chinese economy over the course of the past two decades.

*So, China has proven superior to America because the ends justify the means. People's rights might be trampled on, but the economy is roaring.* The average American would find such an argument revolting, but this is the mindset of most in Silicon Valley.

He then goes on to provide an in-depth analysis of his observations:

> The Bay Area . . . is infested by a bizarre free market-corporatist scientism, "rationalism," a worldview which valorizes laissez-faire economics and "innovation" and distrusts democratic process, all while pretending at neutrality. Those who subscribe to it proudly reject political theory; in their eyes doing so makes them free from the divisions that characterize our political scene, and allows them to posture as purely rational thinkers who arrive at non-political decisions. By

implication, all other policy proposals, those from people with explicit political or philosophical commitments, are irrational, arrived at because they serve political interests, not because the proposals are worthwhile.

**The figures who loom largest in the Bay Area are just as bad, if not worse. They are rarely shy to weigh in on political matters, their confidence buoyed by their belief that their *wealth is indicative of their brilliance* and the *continued fetishization of "STEM"* (science, technology, engineering, and mathematics).** (Emphasis added.)

So, these master technologists believe they are far above making worldview and ethical decisions based on political theories or philosophical/religious texts. Clearly, they are right about…well…just about everything because they have the money to prove it, and they are the messianic embodiment of "STEM." If only they were "just narcissistic," they might cause some ruckus but would otherwise be harmless; however, along with their stratospheric egos, they have the money, brains, and power to make their godlike dreams a reality. This is terrifying, especially considering that their absolutisms go against what many mainstream Americans believe.[19]

# Chapter FOUR
## AI: The Greatest Religion of Them All

"In a few years, there might be religions that are actually correct. Just think about a religion whose holy book is written by AI. That could be a reality in a few years."
Yuval Harari
"Humanity is Not That Simple."
(YouTube. June 6, 2023. Video.)

Not only do these IT creators esteem their creations—and ultimately, themselves—to godlike status and their creating a heavenly utopia, but so do the outside elitists that worship them.

Out of many, Yuval Harari stands out as a thunderous voice, esteeming the new "techno-religion" AI. Although his essay is titled "Salvation by Algorithm: God, Technology, and the New 21st-Century Religions," its essence lies in the subtitle: **"With its world-changing inventiveness,** *technology has become the force religion once was."*[20] (Emphasis added.)

Yuval Harari is a highly regarded philosopher, ethicist, and futurist. He is a secular Jew and a lecturer at Hebrew University in Israel. He is also an anti-religious atheist who believes that sacred creeds and tenants have only held society back from achieving true greatness. After proclaiming that, "God is dead—it just takes awhile to get rid of the body,"[21] he lays his premise on how technology can actually "deliver the goods" instead of where organized religion has always fallen short:

> Nowadays, the most interesting place in the world from a religious perspective is not Syria or the Bible Belt, but Silicon Valley. That is where **hi-tech gurus are brewing for us** *amazing new religions* **that have** *little to do with God,* **and** *everything to do with technology.* **They promise all the old prizes**–happiness, peace, justice and eternal life in paradise–*but here on earth with the help of technology, rather than after death and with the help of supernatural beings.* (Emphasis added.)

Harari argues how religion has always kept people bound to the false belief of eternal destiny—follow a specific path and be destined for heaven; diverge from the "straight and narrow" and burn in hell forever—instead of having the freedom to explore new paths and ideas. AI, he states, offers this new alternative, providing real opportunities to grow and prosper—in the here and now—beyond our wildest dreams. He sarcastically quotes Deuteronomy 11:13-17 where God tells the Israelites that if they obey His commandments, He will bless the fruits of their labor. He will give them bountiful crops and livestock so that "you will eat and be satisfied." If, however, they stray from His edicts by "worship[ping] other gods and bow[ing] down to them . . . the LORD's anger will blaze against you . . . and you will soon perish from the good land the LORD is giving you." Except, **God is actually dead,** says both Nietzsche and Harari, and therefore cannot provide sustenance as He "supposedly" promised. *Science, however, can* through "artificial fertilisers (sic), industrial insecticides and genetically modified crops" in ways that would be unfathomable to the "ancient farmers" who relied only on their gods. He further makes his point by citing modern-day Israel's desalination of the Mediterranean Sea, allowing its desert-dwelling citizens to drink abundant fresh, clean water.[22] *God didn't do that; humankind and its creative genius did that. Again, God is dead, after all.*

Harari further explains:

> New technologies ***kill old gods*** and give ***birth*** to ***new*** gods. . . . [T]he revolutionary technologies of the 21st century are far more likely to **spawn** unprecedented **religious movements** than to **revive medieval creeds. Religions**

that lose touch with the technological realities of the day forfeit their ability even to understand the questions being asked.[23] (Emphasis added.)

Harari claims that *old religious dogmas cannot answer* the questions we will all soon be asking:

> What will happen to the **job market** once artificial intelligence outperforms people in most cognitive tasks? What will be the **political impact** of a vast new class of economically useless people? What will happen to **relationships, families and pension funds** when nanotechnology and regenerative medicine **turn 80 into the new 50?** What will happen to human society when biotechnology enables us to have **designer babies** and to open unprecedented **gaps between rich and poor** and between the remaining productive class and the new useless class?[24]
>
> You will not find the answers to any of these urgent questions in the Quran or sharia law, nor in the Bible and the Confucian Analects, because nobody in the medieval Middle East nor anyone in ancient China knew much about computers, genetics, or nanotechnology.

Again, per Harari, religion has always promised a good game but has never produced any worthwhile goods.

But he then argues that things started to change in the 19th century when "a handful of engineers, politicians, financiers, and visionaries," guided by science and limitless aspirations, proved they could make the unthinkable, thinkable through the Industrial Revolution and influenced by the genius, revolutionary philosophies of that day.[25] He notes, "When we think of 19th-century visionaries, we are far more likely to recall Karl Marx, Friedrich Engels and Vladimir Lenin than the Mahdi, Pius IX or Hong Xiuquan (sic)."

Why? Because unlike these religious prophets:

> **Marx and Lenin were *relevant* to their time.** They studied new technologies and novel economic structures instead of pursuing ancient texts. **The needs, hopes, and fears of the new urban proletarian class were *simply too different from those of biblical peasants*.** To answer these needs, hopes, and fears, Marx and Lenin studied how a steam engine functions, how a coal mine operates, how railroads shape the economy, and how electricity influences politics. (Emphasis added.)

According to Harari, religious teachings should, therefore, be relegated to the damfool, for, as demonstrated by "Marx and his followers, [they] understood the new technological and economic realities. They had relevant answers to the new problems of industrialised (sic) society, as well as original ideas about how to benefit from unprecedented affinities."[26] These socialists were on the right side of history, "**creat[ing]** a *brave new religion for a brave new world*. They promised *salvation through technology and economics*, thus establishing the *first techno-religion in history* and *changing the foundations of human discourse.*"

With this newly established, materialistic religion, people in the *early 20th century* found "questions of technology and economic production **far more ... important than questions about the soul and the afterlife.** In the *second half* of the 20th century, humankind . . . began thinking about technology and production *much more* carefully *than* about *God*."²⁷ (Emphasis added.)

Harari premises that past scientific and technological breakthroughs, along with those who demonstrated how they best be implemented in society, should be idolized, not those ancient texts, philosophers, and prophets that *"stupidly"* claimed they held the meaning to life. They, not Abraham, Moses, Jesus, Mohammed, the Buddha, or Gandhi, are our sacred forebearers.

> Ask yourself: **"What was the most *influential* discovery, invention or creation of the 20th century?"** This is difficult to answer, because it is hard to choose from among a *long list* of candidates, including scientific discoveries such as antibiotics, technological inventions such as computers and ideological creations such as feminism. Now ask yourself: **"What was the most *influential* discovery, invention or creation *of religions* such as Islam and Christianity in the 20th century?" This, too, is difficult, because there is so *little to choose* from.** What did priests, rabbis and mullahs discover in the 20th century that can be mentioned in the same breath as antibiotics, computers or feminism? **Having mulled over these two questions, whence do you think the big changes of the 21st century will emerge: from Islamic State, or from Google?** Yes, ISIS knows how to upload video clips to YouTube. Wow. But, leaving aside the industry of torture, what new inventions have emerged from Syria or Iraq lately? (Emphasis added.)

He then closes his piece with his vision for the future:

> Just as socialism took over the world by promising salvation through steam, so in the coming decades *new techno-religions* **are likely to** *take over the world* **by promising salvation through algorithms and genes.** In the 21st century we will create more powerful myths and more totalitarian religions than in any previous era. **With the help of biotechnology and computer algorithms these religions will not only** *control* **our minute-by-minute existence, but will be able to** *shape* **our bodies, brains and minds and to** *create* **entire virtual worlds, complete with hells and heavens.** (Emphasis added.)

Although Harari's piece disgusts and saddens me, it should be taken seriously. Without realizing it, since the COVID quarantine, we have become much more isolated from each other as individuals, all while the world seems to become smaller. We have replaced human interaction with what our smart devices can offer us. We've lost sight of the transcendent, the wonder, the awe, and the mystery of life. Religious affiliations have given way to the "nones," and such attendance and practice to many have become a thing of the past. We once looked in "awesome wonder" at raw nature and were inspired by it. Now, we would rather keep clicking through social media reels and get our dopamine kick. Why hold meetings in person when we can now provide them virtually? Although we may lose the value of human interaction and productivity, its convenience outweighs all other factors. All the while, technologists and their compatriots continue to build their Tower of Babel towards the heavens where, through their machines, they will be able to control and manipulate us through pleasure and convenience in ways we will never realize; as noted, they already are, but in the future at even grander scales.[28]

So, what about those who see through the utopian façade and refuse to comply? If the paradigm does not shift, it will end up being social Darwinism, a "survival of the fittest" on a much larger scale; either keep up or get run over. The train will continue to roll at an even more rapid speed. At its wheel will be very progressive, elitist technologists and their joint agents who are antithetical to Christian "*hatemongers*" whom they believe want to pull the emergency brake. Therefore, **they must take <u>all means necessary</u> to *stop them*** from destroying their creations. What these narcissists refuse to admit, however, although they know the risk they're taking, is that those AI entities—their Frankenstein creations—will likely evolve into something so big and powerful it will overtake them, too.[29] "Be sure your sin will find you out." (Numbers 32:23 KJV21)

# Part_TWO

# Chapter FIVE

## Fear of Man or Faith in God?

"The Lord is my light and my salvation;
Whom shall I fear? The Lord is the strength
of my life; Of whom shall I be afraid?"
(Psalm 27:1 KJV21)

## Dire and Hopeless

So far, it seems that the future is dire and hopeless. AI and its creators will ensure a utopia, at least from how they view such a society. With its likely evolution into Artificial Superintelligence (ASI), in which these created machines become enlightened enough to surpass even the most intelligent of humans to become a Singleton[30], such attained power could quickly force everyone to follow its decrees or be terminated. Ironically, this will also include the Silicon Valley technologists who had malevolently used AI in an attempt to control humanity themselves. The creators will, therefore, be overtaken by the creation.[31]

But God has a plan. The Old Testament provides stories of how God turned the rebellious Israelites over to their captors to call them back to Him alone; however, He does not leave the captors blameless but judges them for their actions. Ultimately, despite what could have otherwise seemed the end, God always turned things in a specific direction for His glory, leading to the culmination of Christ the Messiah, bringing salvation to the world.

From our Church Fathers until today, there have been many times when the Light has been all but completely snuffed out; however, God has always been faithful to provide the wind of His Holy Spirit to fan the flame. When all seemed lost, the Gospel continued to go forth into all the nations with lives transformed for His Glory. And it still does even now, despite how multitudes of Christians in other countries are being persecuted and martyred for their faith. Although those churches could close their doors and their witness, leaving the once alive Church an empty shell, they haven't. In fact, despite the Enemy's desire to scare them into submission, it has emboldened them, leading others to join them by faith.

God has a plan. He has always had a plan. He promised that before He returned again, the Gospel would be proclaimed to every tribe and nation. Nothing is going to get in the way of that. Nothing is going to stop His mighty hand.

*God has always been faithful to provide the wind of His Holy Spirit to fan the flame.*

## A Ragtag Bunch of Losers

So, it would be very easy to live in fear as Silicon Valley builds its own Tower of Babel towards the heavens. Their seeming desire is for the world to bow down and worship them and their AI machines and overtake anyone—any Christian who stands against them. If this would happen—if God sat back and let them have their way—then there would be no hope for the future. Although the Church is Heaven's ambassador to Earth, AI's unlimited intelligence and resources could quickly destroy it and, therefore, the promulgation of the Gospel.

Interestingly, although they see themselves as saviors to the world, they are frightened, namely, of Christians—a ragtag bunch of losers according to society—overtaking them by the power of the Holy Spirit. This sounds like spiritual warfare—good versus evil and spirit-filled versus demon-possessed—because it is spiritual warfare, without a doubt. The good news is that we have read the back of the "Book" and know we win. God will not be mocked and will have the last word.

In the Tower of Babel account, the Holy Trinity fully knows what's happening. If its builders succeed in their maniacal plans, God's plan of salvation would be stopped then and there. He wouldn't let that happen and knew the only way to stop it was to create language barriers. And, so He did, and there was chaos. Whereas they were on the road to "making a name" for themselves by building the tower to end all towers, they immediately had to abandon ship and scatter in different directions.

## Global Citizens

Throughout history, many dictators and groups have tried to construct their own towers, but no one has been able to come close. Likely, this has been due to many factors, including the infamous "language barrier," as already discussed; also, a lack of resources, finances, power, and intelligence.

In today's 21$^{st}$ century, however, things are on a different playing field. We are all now global citizens, meaning that we are much more interconnected than ever before; the world continues to grow smaller through networking and international business ventures, and it's an everyday occurrence to board a plane and jet off to anywhere in the world at any time.

All these things were unheard of even decades ago. There are also rapid technological breakthroughs that seem extraordinary until the next day when they are outdone by something better. Now, with AI added to the mix, overtaking everything else and obtaining new skills and knowledge at lightning speed, it is logically feasible for how another Tower of Babel could be effectively constructed if allowed to do so.

## Tower of Babel 2.0

But, as it was then, so it will be now. God is actively watching "the city and the tower, which the children of man [are building]." (Gen. 13:5 ESV) He is well aware that these

## Is the Church Ready?

AI developers, their financers, and their influencers "have all one language, and this is only the beginning of what they will do." (v. 6) Soon, he will say, *"Enough!"* and will "confuse their language, so that they might not understand one another's speech." (v. 7)

It's hard to imagine that God will give them fair warning, as they likely have multiple safeguards in place; if something in their system crashes, it can otherwise be fixable. This will continue, and continue, and continue until they finally reach their objective to "make a name for [themselves]." (v. 4) No, God will ensure that **everyone** knows He is "the Lord, and there is no other; apart from me there is no God." (Isaiah 45:5 NIV) Although no human may know where the "off switch" is on AI (or if there is one will soon be overridden by the machine itself), God does; soon He will throw it, everything will come to complete stop, and this tower the "children of man [had] built" (v. 5) will come tumbling down.

It would undoubtedly beg to question what might be the catalyst to shut down IT and AI. Indeed, that is even more of a mystery. Like anyone, I can speculate, but I am confident that it will be earth-shattering. And, just like those at the Tower of Babel likely experienced utter chaos when God ended their shenanigans, it will be this way but on a much larger, global scale. If humanity is already interwoven with technology, whether we like to admit it or not, suddenly, being without it will be as though a part of ourselves will be missing. More than that, however, all these things we depend on daily—from electrical power to daily financial transactions to security monitoring—will cease and desist. The only ones who will be relatively unscathed by this are those who live off the grid, "preppers," or Amish.

## The Body of Christ

### *Desperation and Chaos*

Now, I could give concrete, step-by-step accountings of what we should do to be prepared for such a disaster: Have extra food and water stockpiled, a generator for backup electricity, and a bunker to escape to. Those things are significant; however, the point I'm driving at goes much deeper—that of the soul.

Today's culture finds its most solace in technological conveniences, so much so that it absorbs us. (Hence, the greater concern is how much more taken over we will become as technology and AI advance.) Furthermore, we already look to it as our savior, the answer to our problems. Whereas religious faith was something people depended on in their everyday lives, now they believe they can find the answers to life's deepest challenges, along with solace, happiness, and freedom through what they watch or engage with online. **The only ones** who *truly* **have the answer to life's mysteries**—although sadly, many of those same people have lost sight of this—**are Christians.** We know that the answer to life's ultimate purpose and destiny does not lie in anything else but our relationship with Christ. Nothing is more important; nothing is more life-changing; nothing provides more certainty, grounding, or a sense of peace that is unexplainable amid deepest sufferings. Jesus alone is the answer.

When the bottom falls out, people will want to know where to turn or what to do. They will be frightened, confused, and feel a profound loss. In response, there may be a quick escalation of violence, riots, blaming, and finger-pointing. Often, when such events happen, a person (or anti-Christ type figure) will step in to take charge and claim to have the power to fix things, all the while taking advantage of and exploit people for their own gain, power, and benefit; Hitler is one example of this. And indeed, there will come a day when one, possessed by Satan, will set himself as ruler of the world and destroy anyone that does not bow down and worship him. Praise God; we know what happens to him in the end!

## *Redemption and Revival*

What a time, though, to be a Christian. What a time to help bring in the sheaves. As the Church, we are His hands and feet to make that happen. He certainly doesn't need our help, but as His servants, He allows us the joy of leading people to "the way and the truth and the life." (John 14:6 NIV)

I further see a worldwide Holy Spirit outpouring rivaling the time of Pentecost, and furthermore believe that we have already begun seeing such manifestations starting at the beginning of this year. I believe miracles will become more commonplace as people will be desperate for them. Specifically, I foresee an increase in miraculous healings, especially since access to medical care will be lacking. And this will not only apply to first-world countries but also to those second and third-world places that are without such access even now. But, the greatest miracle of all will be those from all walks of life—young, old, rich, and poor—who realize their need for a Savior and accept for themselves the greatest gift ever offered—eternal, abundant life.

# Chapter SIX
## Are We Ready?

"Now while the Bridegroom was delayed, they all began to nod off, and they fell asleep. But at midnight there was a shout, 'Look! The Bridegroom [is coming]! Go out to meet him.'"
(Matthew 25:6 AMP)

## Is the Church Ready?

Therefore, now comes the biggest question of them all, particularly for the Church: **Are we ready?**

Are we going about our lives deeply rooted and fully surrendered to God, prepared to face anything that might come our way, or are we "riding the fence" with the world and focusing on things temporary versus things eternal? It doesn't mean we shouldn't necessarily stop our typical life routines, but always keep our eyes, ears, and hearts focused toward heaven because we never know when we're expected to go into battle. And this will be the biggest battle of our lives, bar none.

## Prepared or Procrastinating?

I liken this to Jesus' Parable of the Ten Virgins. Although solid theologians have had difficulty interpreting this story, almost all of them would agree it has to do with the Second Coming. My use of the text does *not* concern the rapture or even "final judgment day," so, therefore, may be at risk of being out of context, but its principles still apply. As cited from the Amplified translation:

> Then the kingdom of heaven will be like ten virgins, who took their lamps and went to meet the Bridegroom. Five of them were foolish [thoughtless, silly, and careless], and five were wise [far-sighted, practical, and sensible]. For when the foolish took their lamps, they did not take any [extra] oil with them,

but the wise took flasks of oil along with their lamps. Now while the Bridegroom was delayed, they all began to nod off, and they fell asleep. But at midnight there was a shout, 'Look! The Bridegroom [is coming]! Go out to meet him.' Then all those virgins got up and put their own lamps in order [trimmed the wicks and added oil and lit them]. But the foolish virgins said to the wise, 'Give us some of your oil, because our lamps are going out.' But the wise replied, 'No, otherwise there will not be enough for us and for you, too; go instead to the dealers and buy oil for yourselves.' But while they were going away to buy oil, the Bridegroom came, and those who were ready went in with him to the wedding feast; and the door was shut and locked. Later the others also came, and said, 'Lord, Lord, open [the door] for us.' But He replied, 'I assure you and most solemnly say to you, I do not know you [we have no relationship].' Therefore, be on the alert [be prepared and ready], for you do not know the day nor the hour [when the Son of Man will come]. (Matthew 25:1-13)

To me, John Piper has provided the most sensible explanation of this parable.[32] All ten virgins would be considered followers of Jesus; they are all pure and unblemished. They are not to be regarded as making up the "final" bride of Christ, meaning those Christians still alive on earth when He returns. Instead, their roles are to proclaim the Bridegroom's arrival and follow Him to the wedding.

At first, these virgins readily expected the Bridegroom's coming at any minute. Some of them, however, were more ready than others and therefore were prepared with extra oil to light their lamps; the others, for whatever reason, chose to do without. Later, it says they all fell asleep, which has led many to consider that a negative thing; indeed, in some scriptural contexts, it could be regarded as such. Here, however, at least according to Piper, sleep is to be considered literal and just a part of life's existence:

> Sleep signifies normal, ordinary day-in, day-out life of doing what you got to do and sleeping when you get tired, getting up, doing what you got to do, sleeping when you get tired, getting up, doing what you got to do, going to bed, get the rest you need, get up, do what you got to do. This little word they all slept means what God expects of us in this period of time between the engagement and the marriage is: Do your duty and get the rest you need to do it.[33]

Then, and as a surprise, they were awakened to the news that "the Bridegroom [is coming]! Go out and meet him." (v. 8) All of them got up to go, except the foolish virgins realized they had done a dumb thing; they didn't bring enough oil to keep their lamps lit and therefore couldn't see in the darkness. The wise ones, however, were well-prepared and filled their lamps to see. In the end, the well-prepared wise ones were welcomed inside the marriage feast to enjoy its lavish festivities. The foolish ones, however, arrived late to the party and could not be found on the guest list.

## Well Oiled or Dried Up?

Piper wraps his sermon with a beautiful invitation:

> Are you ready? Do you have oil in the form of your religion? Life, faith, hope, love, reali-

ty, or are you just carrying your formal little lamp around? "I go to Church. I carry a Bible. I pray before meals. I try to keep the Ten Commandments." Your little lamp. But inside, nothing of spiritual affections for God, love for the Bridegroom, an intense expectancy that it is going to be better when he comes than the best sex you ever had or the best food you ever had or the best success you ever had. No life like that.[34]

As followers of Christ, we should not live in fear of the future or keep our eyes so fixed to heaven that we are of no earthly good. It does mean, however, to ensure that our lamps are filled with the oil of the Holy Spirit; to be ready in and out of season to preach the Gospel (2 Timothy 4:2); to not spend all our time navel gazing or even more specific, glued to our smartphones. Everything should be in moderation while always loving Him with all our hearts, souls, and minds.

### Greater Things to Come

God has something beyond comprehension in store and is ready to use the Church to make it happen. He is eager to use us as His hands and feet to provide comfort, healing, and the Gospel message to those most averse to hearing about it. He is ready to pour out his Spirit and do miracle after miracle.

He wants to show the world who He is, and He wants His followers to be the ones to do it. How humbling, thrilling, overwhelming, and exciting it is to be Christ's ambassadors, especially during a time like this, that He wants us to "prepare the way of the Lord." He will only use us if we

## Is the Church Ready?

prepare ourselves to be used. We must die to ourselves and fully surrender before Him. Then, in that death, He will raise us up and fill us to overflowing through the power of the Holy Spirit. We no longer have to drink the spiritual milk of infants and children. We must step into the spiritual adults that we are and eat the meat of the deeper life (cf. 1 Cor. 3: 2-6).

God is ready to do more in us, from the most recent of converts to the most seasoned of disciples. He wants to use us to turn the world right side up when it is turned upside down. He wants us to be part of the wise virgins who, when He calls, are already prepared and ready to go. He is preparing a feast from His bountiful harvest. He wants us to have the best seats at the table to give thanks and partake in His goodness.

**May we not be found lacking when He comes.**

## Is the Church Ready?
### *Endnotes*

1 "The ziggurat represents the cosmic mountain on which God or the gods dwell. The priest's ascent up the stairway to the temple at the top of the ziggurat represents the ascent to heaven. The top of the ziggurat was crowned by a temple containing the statue of the god. Ziggurats thus provided the link between heaven and earth, allowing humans to ritually ascend into the presence of God. (In this regard, Jacob's vision of the 'ladder' (Hebrew 'sullam') or, better, 'stairway' into heaven (Genesis 28:10-22) matches the symbolism of the ziggurat.)" – As cited in Hamblin, William, and Daniel Peterson. "Ziggurats Are Temple Platforms of Ancient Mesopotamia."; Deseret News. June 17, 2013. https://www.deseret.com/2013/6/17/20521225/ziggurats-are-temple-platforms-of-ancient-mesopotamia.

2 "The Tower of Babel incident occurred around 4,200 years ago—about 100 years after the Flood but before Abraham was born. This was before ancient Egypt, Greece, and other early civilizations. These places couldn't have begun until other people left Babel to establish these other civilizations." – As cited in "In what Time Period of the Tower of Babel Built in?"; Answers in Genesis. August 24, 2017. https://answersingenesis.org/kids/bible/babel/what-time-period-was-babel/.

3 Wikipedia cites the eras of technology to be Prehistorical, Ancient, Medieval, Industrial Revolution (1760-1860s), Second Industrial Revolution (1860s-1947), Third Industrial or "Digital" Revolution (1947-2015), and the Fourth Industrial or "Imagination" Revolution (2015-present). https://en.wikipedia.org/wiki/History_of_technology

4 Ng, Joanna. "How Artificial Intelligence Is Today's Tower of Babel"; Christianity Today. June 17, 2020. https://www.christianitytoday.com/ct/2020/june-web-only/artificial-intelligence-todays-tower-of-babel-ai-ethics.html.

5 I can hardly understand computers or smart devices, to start with, so to me, this comes from a whole other galaxy. Therefore, although I address this topic with trepidation and admit ignorance, I also know that even those more competent than me have difficulty comprehending this concept.

6 Marc Andreessen. "Why AI Will Save the World"; Substack. June 6,

2023. https://pmarca.substack.com/p/why-ai-will-save-the-world.

7 Ibid.

8 Andreessen 2023

9 Ibid.

10 Ibid.

11 Andreessen 2023

12 Kadaras, Nicholas. 2022. Digital Madness: How Social Media Is Driving Our Mental Health Crisis--and How to Restore Our Sanity. St. Martin's Press.

13 "Amid concerns surrounding the emergence of new technology, evangelist Nick Vujicic is making a case that artificial intelligence and digital media can play pivotal roles in spreading the Gospel to diverse audiences worldwide. [His] latest initiative, "Multitood", seeks to expand the Kingdom's impact through cutting-edge technology and digital content creation. [This] software translates [Gospel] videos into more than 36 languages, adds and edits subtitles and natural-sounding voiceovers [that are streamed] over the Internet." – As cited in Klett, Leah M. "Nick Vujicic Unveils AI-Powered Solution to Spread the Gospel Globally: "We Can Use It for the Kingdom." The Christian Post. July 29, 2023. https://www.christianpost.com/news/nick-vujicic-unveils-ai-powered-solution-to-spread-gospel.html.

14 Ng 2023.

15 Manjoo, Farid. "Silicon Valley's Politics: Liberal, with One Big Exception." The New York Times. September 6, 2017. https://www.nytimes.com/2017/09/06/technology/silicon-valley-politics.html.

16 Ibid.

17 Henley, Wallace B. 2021. Who Will Rule the Coming Gods? Vide Press.

18 Baron, Noah. "Silicon Valley's Poverty of Philosophy." Huffington Post. July 27, 2017. https://www.huffpost.com/entry/silicon-valleys-poverty-of-philosophy_b_59792e64e4b0c69ef7052571.

19 Henley 2021

20 Harari, Yuval. "Salvation by Algorithm: God, Technology and the New 21st-Century Religions."; The New Statesman. September 9,

## Is the Church Ready?

2016. https://www.newstatesman.com/politics/2016/09/salvation-by-algorithm-god-technology-and-the-new-21st-century-religions.

21 Ibid.

22 "A mere 14 years after its government sounded the alarm on a growing water crisis, Israel is moving rapidly toward a sustainable water future. The country now draws and desalinates 75 percent of its drinking water from the Mediterranean Sea. And where the US reclaims just 4 percent of its wastewater for agricultural purposes, Israel repurposes nearly 90 percent." – As cited in Lindell, Rebecca. "A Closer Look at How Israel Manages Its Precious Water Resources."; Northwestern Now. October 19, 2022. https://news.northwestern.edu/stories/2022/10/global-engineering-trek-israel-water/#:~:text=The%20country%20now%20draws%20and,Israel%20repurposes%20nearly%2090%20percent.

23 Harari 2016

24 These questions are not a pipe dream but are valid, especially if society continues its current trajectory. Numerous sources say that we will face these ethical dilemmas sooner than anticipated. What is even more stunning, however, is that the "gods of Silicon Valley" will likely be providing solutions vastly different from mainstream American, centrist values.

25 Ibid.

26 Ibid.

27 Ibid.

28 Kadaras 2022

29 Bryk, William. "Artificial Superintelligence: The Coming Revolution." Harvard Science Review. Accessed August 7, 2023. http://harvardsciencereview.com/artificial-superintelligence-the-coming-revolution/.

30 "In futurology, a *singleton* is a hypothetical world order in which there is a single decision-making agency at the highest level, capable of exerting effective control over its domain, and permanently preventing both internal and external threats to its supremacy. The term was first defined by [Swedish philosopher] Nick Bostrom." As cited in Wikipedia. 2023. "Singleton (Global Governance)." Wikimedia Foundation. Last modified August 12, 2023. https://en.wikipedia.org/wiki/

Singleton_(global_governance)

31 Bryk 2023

32 Piper, John. "The End Is near - Are You Ready?" Desiring God. June 29, 2016. https://www.desiringgod.org/interviews/the-end-is-near-are-you-ready.

33 Ibid.

34 Ibid.

## Appendix

I WANTED TO RECOMMEND TWO RESOURCES from which I drew highly while writing this book. Unlike myself, these authors are esteemed scholars and experts in their fields. Therefore, I find it befitting to recognize them and their works for others to glean from:

- *Who Will Rule the Coming 'Gods'? The Looming Spiritual Crisis of Artificial Intelligence* is written by Dr. Wallace B. Henley, a pastor and expert in Christian worldview formation. Endorsed by several high-level scholars and professionals, his book compares the transcendent God of the universe and the imminent 'gods of Silicon Valley.' He further details how AI technologists hold secularly humanistic and radically progressive worldviews that drive them to change the world, much the opposite of Judeo-Christian mores.

- *Digital Madness: How Social Media is Driving our Mental Health Crisis—and How to Restore Our Sanity* is written by Dr. Nicholas Kadaras, a renowned clinical psychologist and forerunner in understanding and treating internet addiction. His book explains how social media use is rewiring our brains to be increasingly dependent on it, drawing us towards isolation and polarization from others by fear and black-and-white thinking, and making us more prone to acute mental disorders, substance abuse, body dysmorphia, non-lethal self-harm (i.e., cutting, etc.), and ultimately, suicide. Furthermore, Kadaras is not afraid to call out the world-renowned social media giant CEOs (e.g., Zuckerberg, Gates, Bezos, etc.) and explore each of their deep narcissistic drives for godlike power through their own confessions. Note that this book is not Christian-based, but the information he provides is invaluable in understanding AI's psychological underpinnings.

Also listed are expounded citations:

- "God is not a genie in a bottle, and your wish is not His command. His command better be your wish." Batterson, Mark. *Circle Maker*. Zondervan, 2016.

- "To infinity, and beyond!" Buzz Lightyear. *Toy Story*. Film. United States: Walt Disney Studios Pixar, 1995.

- Poor man wanna be rich, rich man wanna be king, and a king ain't satisfied til he rules everything." Bruce Springsteen. *Badlands. Darkness on the Edge of Town*. The Record Plant, New York: Sony Music Entertainment, 1978.

- "In a few years, there might be religions that are actually correct. Just think about a religion whose holy book is written by AI. That could be a reality in a few years." Yuval Noah Harari. "Humanity is Not That Simple." YouTube video. June 6, 2023. https://youtu.be/4hIlDiVDww4?si=o-pz9EPd6_Fx7ZLL

- Kubrick, Stanley, director. *2001: A Space Odessy*. April 2, 1968; Stanley Kubrick Productions, 1968. 139 minutes. film.

# Acknowledgements

ALTHOUGH I HAVE BEEN AFFORDED MANY OPPORTUNITIES and have accomplished much, my most valued treasures are those who have influenced my life. Some are close friends and family; others are acquaintances. Some are still part of my life, while others have moved on. Some are still on this side of eternity, while others have already crossed. There are even those I have never met in person; the lives they lived have helped shape me into the person I am today. Though they all deserve recognition, I have listed only a few of them below for the sake of brevity:

TO MY WIFE, MY SOULMATE, MY LIFELONG companion, and the only person I know who could ever put up with my flaws and inadequacies: Thank you for loving me deeply and teaching me the concepts of grace, liberty, and unconditional love. I could never imagine nor want my life apart from you.

TO MY DAUGHTER, WHO HAS MADE ME SO PROUD, I'm busting at my seams: You have the most compassionate heart for others and love Jesus. If there's nothing more I could have ever taught you, these two things are more important than everything else.

TO MY FATHER AND PATERNAL GRANDFATHER, WHO HAVE SINCE PASSED on to their eternal reward: They will always be my heroes. They taught me the value of hard work, determination, perseverance, choosing to find joy in life's darkest moments, and how to "be a man." I look forward to seeing you both again someday.

TO MY MOTHER, WHO HAS AMAZED ME WITH HER DETERMINATION and perseverance despite life's obstacles: Your desire to win others for Christ and your commitment to prayer have impacted me deeply. Thank you for your "mother's love" which you give to me and your daughter-in-law and granddaughter.

TO MY BLOOD RELATIVES, OF WHOM I SEE the shared traits of self-sacrifice, grit, and bullheadedness: We clearly are cut from the same cloth! I thank God for all of you, especially the ones who have chosen to seek the Kingdom of God first. May "the circle be unbroken in the sky."

To my marital relatives, who have welcomed me with open arms as one of your own: Not only did I gain a wife, but also parents, grandparents, brothers, sisters, aunts, uncles and cousins. I love you all.

To my best friend, who has been closer than a brother to me for over 30 years: It's incredible how, despite the past years of physical distance between us, we are once again living near each other, and our wives and kids are now also good friends. God has always had a plan for our friendship, and I believe there's still more to come.

To my pastors, both past and present: I am grateful to have been under your leadership and teachings and led by the examples you have set in service to Christ. Even more, I've been blessed to have become very close with a few of you, having walked alongside me during very dark times. Great is your reward in heaven!

To my former teachers and professors: Thank you for equipping me to think critically and shaping my worldview. Your guidance prepared me for my professional career and left me with a zeal for lifelong learning.

To my heroes of the faith, including Mother Teresa, Archbishop Oscar Romero, and Dietrich Bonhoeffer: Your legacies brought about pivot points in my life, shaped who I am today, and are who I want to model after as a Christian. I look forward to meeting you all someday in heaven, thanking you for all you meant to me, and engaging you in long conversations.

Although I don't know how often such recognition is given in book acknowledgments, I want to thank the authors of the articles I researched and cited in writing this book. Although I intensely disagree with some of you, I am grateful for all your voices in challenging my presumptions and helping shape my beliefs and understanding of this complicated subject.

Last but certainly not least, I WANT TO THANK MY PUBLISHER, STELLA SOTO-CRAWFORD, and her company, Take Heart Books. I will always be amazed and humbled at your willingness to share my message with a broader audience simply because you believed in its importance. May God turn your dreams into realities.

# About Adam R. Hunter

ALTHOUGH HE HAS SPENT MUCH OF HIS CAREER in mental health and crisis intervention, Adam has always been interested in how sociocultural and political changes intersect with Christianity. He believes that before another Great Awakening can happen, the Church must make itself right before God and experience its own revival.

Adam is a Licensed Independent Social Worker in the State of Ohio and is a crisis therapist. He holds a Bachelor of Arts degree in psychology from Mount Vernon Nazarene University, a Master of Social Work degree from West Virginia University, and, although not currently enrolled, completed several doctoral-level courses in clinical psychology from Regent University. He has also been afforded other exclusive educational opportunities, including attending the Focus Leadership Institute at the Focus on the Family headquarters in Colorado Springs, Colorado, and learning from leading experts in Christian worldview formation.

Adam has been actively involved in church and ministry opportunities since childhood, specifically involving music and short-term mission work throughout the United States and abroad. As a classically trained vocalist, he was blessed to have traveled with the Celebrant Singers, an internationally recognized music ministry, spreading the Good News of the Gospel through song across the United States and Venezuela.

Adam's highest calling is to be a devoted husband and father. With that, he lives with his wife and daughter in North Central Ohio.

Adam can be followed on his blog, where he has written many other relevant pieces:

https://www.medium.com/@adamhunter_76

THANK YOU *for reading this book! I pray that you are seeking His will for your life and are* READY *according to His purpose!*

*God Bless!*

www.ingramcontent.com/pod-product-compliance
Lightning Source LLC
Chambersburg PA
CBHW060853050426
42453CB00008B/966